CCNA Routing and Switching (ICND1 100-105, ICND2 200-105, and CCNA 200-125)

Short guide and additional help to passing your exam

Tags: network protocol, ccna routing and switching, storage area networks, ccna security, ccna cloud, ccna data center, network security, computer networking books, computer networking basics, computer networking for dummies, network devices, network marketing, osi model, ospf.

This book covers the following topics:

*I*ntroduction

Computer networking is very essential. A good example of the power of networking is the internet, which is a global collection of interconnected computers exchanging data with each other. That is what we can achieve with computer networking. However, networks are complex and need individuals with a good technical background in order to manage them. The network devices need to be configured well and secured for the users to enjoy quality services. With the best networking skills, you will become a good network administrator. This book will help you become one.

Chapter 1

Network Fundamentals

A network refers to a group of two more computer devices or systems connected together for the purpose of data sharing. Networks exchange files, share resources and exchange electronic information. For example, networked computers can share a printer or share a file with each other.

Types of Networks

There are a number of computer networks, with the common ones being the following:

- LAN (Local Area Network)- the computer are geographically close to each other, for example, in the same building.
- WAN (Wide Area Network)- the computers are geographically apart and are communicated via radio signals or telephone lines.
- MAN (Metropolitan Area Network) - this is a data network designed for use in a town or city.
- HAN (Home Area Network) - a computer network designed for a home to connect various personal devices.
- VPN (Virtual Private Network) - a computer network constructed by use of public wires, mostly the internet, to connect to a private network like a company's internal network.
- SAN (Storage Area Network) - this is a high speed network for storage devices that also connects the same devices to servers.

Network Standards

Network standards help ensure that network hardware and software work together. Without such standards, it would be difficult to develop a network for sharing information. Network standards can be *formal* or *informal (de facto)*. The formal standards are developed by governments or industry organizations. Such standards exist for data link layer, network layer software, hardware etc.

The formal standardization is a very lengthy process followed to develop the specification, identify choices and industry acceptance. There are a number of industries for standardization including the popular Internal Organization for Standardization (ISO), The American National Standards Institute (ANSI) etc. Internet Engineering Task Force (IETF) is the most popular organization for standards. It sets standards governing the way the internet operates. The second class of networking standards is the informal (de facto) standards. These are the standards that emerge in the marketing standards and followed by vendors but they don't have any official backing. A good example of a de facto standard is Microsoft Windows, but no standards organization recognizes it. It is only widely recognized and accepted.

Network Components/Devices

There are a number of components that are common to networks. Examples of such devices include the server, clients, transmission media etc. Let us discuss the common network components and devices:

1. Server- this is a computer or any other device responsible for managing the network. Servers are usually dedicated, which means that they don't perform any other tasks other than their server tasks. A server mostly receives requests from the client machines and sends responses to them.
2. Client- this is an application running on a personal computer or a workstation and it relies on the server computer to perform its tasks. It sends requests to the server and gets responses from the server.
3. Devices- these are computer devices like the printer and CD-ROM that are not part of the essential computer. Examples of such devices include printers, modems and disk drives.
4. Transmission media- this is the physical media that carries information from one device to another in the form of signals. Common transmission media include fiber optic cable, coaxial cable and the twisted-pair cable.
5. NOS (Network Operating System) - The BOS has special functions of connecting computers and devices to form a local area network (LAN). The term network operating

system is mostly to refer to software that enhances the basic operating system by adding networking features.

6. Operating System- this is software that provides a platform on which application programs can run. The operating systems are tasked with common tasks like receiving keyboard input from users, tracking files and directories, sending output to the screen and controlling the peripheral devices like printers and disk drives.

7. Network Interface Card (NIC) – this is an expansion card that is connected to a computer for the computer to connect to a network. Many NICs are developed to fit a specific network, media and protocol although there are some of them capable of serving multiple networks.

8. Hub- This marks a common connection point for all devices in a network. A hub comes with numerous ports. After a packet has been received on one port, it is copied to the other ports of the hub so that it may be seen by other network segments.

9. Switch– a device responsible for filtering and forwarding packets between LAN segments. The switches operate at layer 2 (data link layer) and in some cases layer 3 (network layer) of OSI reference model.

10. Router- this is a device for forwarding data packets across networks. A router is normally connected to at least two networks and placed at gateways, which are places where two or more networks connect.

11. Gateway- this is a node on a network serving as an entry point to another network.

12. Bridge- a device for connecting two Local Area Networks (LANS) or two segments of same LAN using the same protocol.

13. Channel Service Unit/Digital Service Unit (CSU/DSU) – A CSU is a device for connecting a terminal to a digital line. Mostly, the two devices are packaged as one unit.

14. Terminal Adapter (ISDN Adapter) – a device for connecting a computer to external digital communications line, like an ISDN line. A terminal adapter is more like a modem but it only needs to pass along digital signals.

15. Access Point- a computer software or hardware device that acts as a communication hub for the users of a wireless device to be able to connect to a wired LAN.
16. Modem (modulator-demodulator) – a program or device that enables a computer to transmit data over cable o telephone lines.
17. Firewall- a system that has been designed and developed to prevent unauthorized access to or from a private network. A firewall implementation can be made up of hardware or software or both.
18. MAC (Media Access Control) Address- this is a unique ID code that is assigned to a network adapter or any device that comes with built-in networking capability.

Network Models

To make networks simple, everything is separated into layers and every layer handles certain tasks and is not dependent of all the other layers. Control is passed from one layer to next layer, beginning from the top layer in one station then proceeds to bottom layer over channel to next station then back up the hierarchy. Network models define the set of network layers and the way they interact.

The two popular network models include:

- TCP/IP Model
- The OSI Network Model

The OSI Model

OSI stands for open systems interconnect (OSI). It is an open standard for communication systems. It is a networking model that implements protocols in seven layers:

1. Physical layer
   This layer is responsible for conveying the bit stream, light, electrical impulse or radio signal throughout the network at mechanical and electrical level. It provides that hardware for sending and receiving data on a carrier including definition

of cards, cables and physical aspects. Examples are Ethernet, B8ZS, V.35, FDDI, V.24, RJ45.

2. Data Link Layer
    This layer is responsible for encoding and decoding data into bits. It handles the errors of the physical layer, frame synchronization and flow control. This layer is further subdivided into two sub-layers, MAC (Media Access Control) and LLC (Logical Link Control).

3. Network Layer
    This is the OSI layer responsible for providing switching and routing technologies and creation of logical paths popularly known as *virtual circuits* for transmission of data from one node to another. This layer is responsible for routing and forwarding tasks. Other tasks of this layer include error handling, internetworking, addressing, and packet sequencing and congestion control.

4. Transport Layer
    This is the layer responsible for transferring data between end systems or hosts and is responsible for flow control end-to-end error recovery. It's responsible for ensuring there is complete data transfer.

5. Session Layer
    This layer is responsible for establishing, managing and terminating connections between applications. The layer sets takes the task of setting up, coordinating and terminating conversations dialogues and exchanges between applications at each end.

6. Presentation Layer
    This layer creates independence from the differences in data presentation (like encryption) by translation of data from application to network format. It also does the vice versa. It also encrypts and formats data for transmission through the network preventing chances of having compatibility problems.

7. Application Layer
    This layer supports end-user and application processes. The quality services and communication partners are identified, user privacy and authentication are considered and any constraints about data syntax are identified. Everything in the layer is treated as being application-specific. It provides

application services to be used for file transfers, email and the other services regarding network software.

The TCP/IP Model

The TCP/IP network model is made up of 4 layers. All protocols belonging to TCP/IP protocol belong to the first/top three layers of this model. Let us discuss these layers:

1. Application
   This layer defines the TCP/IP application protocols and the way host programs interface with the transport layer service to use a network. Examples of protocols operating in this layer include HTTP, Telnet, TFTP, SNMP, FTP, DNS and SMTP.
2. Transport
   This layer is responsible for communication session management as it takes place between host computers. It defines the status of connection and level of service used during transportation of data. Examples of protocols for this layer include TCP, RTP and UDP.
3. Internet
   This layer is responsible for packaging data into datagrams, with source and destination address information which is used for forwarding datagrams between hosts and across the networks. It is responsible for routing_IP datagrams. Examples of internet layer protocols include IP, ARP, ICMP and RARP.
4. Network Interface
   This layer is responsible for specifying the way data is physically transmitted through the network including the way bits electrically signaled by the hardware devices that interface directly with the network medium like optical fiber, coaxial cable or twisted-pair copper wire. Examples of protocols for this layer include Ethernet, Token Ring, X.25, Frame Relay, FDDI, RS-232 and v.35.

Each TCP/IP layer corresponds to one or more of the seven layers of OSI reference model.

Network Topologies

Network topology is the arrangement or shape of various elements in a computer network, that is, the nodes and the links. The network topology determines the way connection between various network nodes is done and how the nodes communicate with each other.

A topology can be either physical or logical. Here are the main topologies that LANs rely on:

1. Bus Topology
   In this topology, all devices are connected to a central cable known as *bus* or *backbone*. It is an easy topology to implement and relatively cheap compared to other network topologies.
2. Ring Topology
   The devices in the network are connected to form a closed loop, meaning that each device is connected to two other devices, one on each side.
3. Star Topology
   There is a central hub to which all devices are connected. They can be installed and managed with much ease. However, bottlenecks may sometimes occur since all the data must pass through the central hub.
4. Tree Topology
   This type of topology combines the characteristics of both star and linear bus topologies. It has a group of star-configured workstations connected to linear bus backbone cable.

It is possible for the above topologies to be mixed. For example, we can have a bus-star topology with a high-bandwidth bus called *backbone* connecting many slower-bandwidth star segments.

Network Architectures

The network architecture includes both the logical and physical design of a network. It includes the network hardware, software, protocols and media for transmitting data. It denotes the way various computers are organized and the tasks or roles each computer plays in the network.

It is the role of the network engineer and other network specialists to design the best architecture of an organization network. Let us discuss the common network architectures:

Peer-to-Peer (P2P)

In this type of network architecture, tasks are allocated to each peer/host/computer on the network. All devices are equal and there is no hierarchy in terms of arrangement of the devices. The computers also have same ability to use the network resources. This type of architecture has no server, which could be a shared resource. Instead, each computer will act as a server for the files that it stores. It will also act as a client in order to get the files stored on the other computer. This type of architecture requires no dedicated server, making it less costly. In case a host fails, the other one(s) will keep on working. The peer-to-peer network architecture is highly supported by the modern operating systems, making it easy for one to install and use.

However, this type of architecture has a number of disadvantages. Back up of data and files must be done on each computer. Also, as more and more devices are added to the P2P network, security, performance and access will become a problem.

Client/Server Architecture

In this type of architecture, a centralized and very powerful computer and to which every other computer connects acts as the hub. The other computers are known as the *clients*. The server acts as the heart of the system, managing and providing resources to the clients on request. The resources and the security of the data are controlled via this server. It is good type of architecture for use when there are several computers unlike the P2P architecture. The servers are also accessible anywhere and across many platforms.

However, this type of architecture is associated with a number of disadvantages. A server and networking resources like routers and switches are needed, which can make the implementation of this architecture expensive. Technical staffs are also needed to ensure that network runs efficiently.

Chapter 2

Network Cabling

Network cables are used to connect computers and facilitate the transfer of data between network devices. There are different cable types and these are designed for different purposes. Let us discuss them:

Coaxial cables

This type of cable is made up of a single copper cable at the center. A plastic layer is used to provide insulation between the copper cable and a braided metal shield. The work of the metal shield is to prevent outside interference that may come from motors, fluorescent lights and other computers.

Coaxial cables are hard to install, but they offer high resistance to signal interference. It is also good in that it can support long cable lengths between the network devices. The coaxial cable is further divided into two:

- Thin coaxial
- Thick coaxial

The thin coaxial is also known as *thinnet*. 10Base2 is a specification for a thin coaxial cable that carries Ethernet signals. The 2 denotes the approximate maximum segment length that is 200 meters. In reality, the actual segment length is 185 meters. It is mostly used in school networks, especially those employing the bus topology.

Thick coaxial cable is also known as *thicknet*. 10Base5 denotes the specifications for a thick coaxial cable that carries Ethernet signals. The 5 denotes maximum segment length which is 500 meters. The thick coaxial cable has an extra plastic cover that keeps moisture away from the central cable. It is a good choice for use as the when implementing a bus topology. However, it is difficult to install since it doesn't bend easily.

Coaxial cables commonly use the BNC (Bayone-Neill-Concelman) connector.

Fiber Optic Cable

The fiber optic cables are made up of a center glass which is surrounded by several layers of protective materials. Instead of transmitting electronic signals, the fiber optic cable transmits light eliminating the danger of electrical interference. This has made the fiber optic a good choice where there are high chances of electrical interference. It is also immune to lighting and moisture, making it a good choice for use in buildings.

The fiber optic cable is capable of transmitting signals over longer distances compared to other choices like twisted pair and coaxial cable. It is also capable of transmitting information at faster speeds, making it a good choice for communications including interactive services and video conferencing. Its cost is most the same to that of copper, but it is hard to install and modify. 10BaseF is a specification for fiber optic cable that carries Ethernet signals.

The center core of the fiber optic cable is made up of plastic or glass fibers. The fiber center is then cushioned by a plastic coating, and a Kevlar fiber helps in strengthening the cable and preventing breakage. Its outer insulating jacket is made of PVC or Teflon.

Twisted Pair Cables

This became popular in the 1990s as the leading cable for Ethernet, beginning with 10 Mbps (10BASE-T, also known as CAT3). It was then followed by 100 Mbps (100BASE-TX, Cat5, and Cat5e). Higher speeds of 10 Gbps (10GBASE-T) were achieved later. The Ethernet twisted pair cables have up to 8 wires which are wound together in pairs to minimize the effect of electromagnet interference.

There are two types of twisted pair cable that are available in the market, that is, Unshielded Twisted Pair (UTP) and the Shielded Twisted Pair (STP). Modern Ethernet cables rely on UTP wiring since it is cheap. The STP cabling is mostly found in other types of networks like Fiber Distributed Data Interface (FDDI). The UTP relies on the RJ-45 as the standard connector. The RJ stands for Registered Jack.

This means that the connector relies on a standard that was imported from the telephone industry. The UTP is the cheapest, but it is prone to electrical and radio frequency interference. If you need to use cables in places with huge potential difference or if you will have to place the cable in sensitive environments that may be affected by the electrical current in UTP, I recommend that you use the twisted pair cable. The shielded cables are good in extending the maximum cable distance.

Crossover Cables

Null modem cables belong to this type. A crossover cable is used for joining two network devices that belong to the same type. Examples are two network switches or PCs.

Crossover cables were commonly used in the early days at homes for connection of individual computers to each other directly. Externally, the Ethernet crossover cables seem to be similar to the ordinary (sometimes referred to as *straight-through)* with the only difference being the order in which the color-codes wires are arranged at the end of the cable connector. Today, most home networks rely on routers with built-in features for cross-over; hence the need for these cables is not much.

Chapter 3

*IPV*4 and *IPv*6 addressing

IP stands for *Internet Protocol*. It specifies the technical format for packets and the addressing scheme to be used by computers for communication over the internet. In most networks, IP is combined with a higher-level protocol known as TCP (transmission Control Protocol) to establish a virtual connection between the source and the destination.

The IP on its own can be seen as the postal system. It helps you in addressing a package and dropping it in the system, but there exists no direct link between you and the recipient. The TCP/IP first establishes a connection between the center and the recipient so that transmission of messages can be done.

Currently, there are two versions of IP, namely *IPV4* and *IPV6*. The latter is the latest and it will remain in the market for some time with the former.

IPV4

This marks the fourth revision of IP protocol. It helps in identifying network devices based on an addressing system. The IP is designed to be used in interconnected systems of the packet-switched communication networks.

IPV4 forms the most widely used internet protocol for connection of computers and other devices to the internet. It relies on a32-bit address system to give 2^{32} addresses (just above 4 billion addresses). Every device that connects to the internet, including computers, smart phones, consoles etc. requires an IP address. The internet is growing each day and the number of unused IPV4 addresses is expected to be depleted.

An IPV4 address takes the x.x.x.x format. The *x* must be a decimal value and its value must range between 0 and 255. The octets are separated by periods. Each IPV4 address must have 4 octets and 3 periods. Here are examples of valid IPV4 addresses:

- 1 . 2 . 3 . 4
- 01 . 103 . 104 . 105

IPV6

The IPV6 addressing scheme was developed to meet the increasing demand for IP addresses. It is also known as *IPng* (Internet Protocol next generation) and it marks the latest version of IP reviewed by IETF standards committees to replace the IPV4 scheme.

IPV6 is the successor of IPV4. It was designed to evolve the internet protocol and it will coexist with its predecessor, IPV4 for some time. This will allow the internet to grow gradually in terms of the number of connecting devices and amount of data that is being transmitted.

An IPV6 address can take any of the following two formats:

- Normal: Pure IPv6 format
- Dual: IPv6 plus IPv4 formats

A normal IPV6 address takes the format given below:

y : y : y : y : y : y : y : y

Each *y* is referred to as a *segment* and it can be any hexadecimal value between o and FFFF. Each segment is separated from the others using a colon (:) rather than a period. A normal IPV6 address is expected to have 8 segments. However, some circumstances allow for the use of short notations. Here are examples of valid normal IPV6 addresses:

- 2001 : db8: 2222 : 4444 : 5555 : 6666 : 7777 : 8888
- 2001 : db8 : 2222 : 4444 : CCCC : DDDD : EEEE : FFFF
- : : (indicates all the 8 segments are zero)
- 2001: db8: : (indicates the last 6 segments are zero)
- : : 1335 : 45678 (indicates that the first 6 segments are zero)
- 2001 : db8: : 2256 : 5678 (indicates the middle 4 segments are zero)

- 2001:0db8:0001:0000:0000:0ab9:C0A8:0102 (We can compress to do away with its leading zeros. We get the following: 2001:db8:1::ab9:C0A8:102)

An IPV6 dual address combines both IPV6 and IPV4 addresses using the format given below:

y : y : y : y : y : y : x . x . x . x

The IPV6 portion of the addresses (denotes by y's) comes first then it is followed by the IPV4 part of the address (denoted by x's).

In the section for IPV6, each y is known as a *segment* and it can be any hexadecimal value between 0 and FFFF. Colons (:) are used to separate the segments rather than periods. The IPV6 part of the address must take 6 segments but there are short notations for zeros.

In the IPV4 section of the address, each x is known as an *octet* and it must be a decimal value ranging between 0 and 255. Periods are used to separate octets. The IPV4 section of the address must have four octets and 4 periods.

Here are some examples of valid IPV6 Dual addresses:

- 2001 : db8: 3333 : 4544 : 5655 : 6566 : 3 . 1 . 2 . 4
- : : 11 . 22 . 33 . 44 (implies all six IPv6 segments are zero)
- 2001 : db8: : 122 . 124 . 124 . 124 (indicates that the last 4 IPv6 segments are zero)
- : : 1235 : 6678 : 81 . 124 . 5 . 56 (indicates that the first 4 IPv6 segments are zero)
- : : 1234 : 5678 : 1 . 1 . 3 . 4 (indicates that the first 4 IPv6 segments are zero)
- 2001 : db8: : 1244 : 5798 : 5 . 6 . 7 . 8 (indicates that the middle 2 IPv6 segments are zero)

IPV4 Subnet Masks

IP addresses are normally subdivided into portions. One portion marks the network (network number) while the other part marks the specific host or machine in the network (host number).

IPV4 relies on subnet masks while IPV6 relies on prefixes to identify the range of hosts making up a subnet, or the group of IP addresses that are on the same network. A subnet can help you identify all hosts within a department, building, and geographic location or in the same LAN. When an organization's network is divided into subnets, it allows the organization to connect to the internet via one shared network address. Subnet masks and prefixes are useful when a host needs to communicate with another system. If the system is running on same subnet or network, it will try to look for that address in the local link. If the system is running on a different network, the packet will first be send to a gateway which will in turn send it to the right address. This type of routing is known as CIDR (Classless-InterDomain Routing). In IPV4, a subnet mask 255.255.255.0 has 32 bits and is made up of four octets, each 8 bits. The IP address 10.10.10.0 with a subnet mask of 255.255.255.0 simply means that the subnet has a range of IP addresses running between 10.10.10.0 - 10.10.10.255. In IPV6, the prefix length is similar to subnet mask in IPV4. However, instead of expressing it in four octets like in IPV4, it is written as an integer between 1 and 128. Consider the following IP address:

2001:db8:abcd:0012::0/64

The above address defines a subnet with the following range of IP addresses:

2001:db8:abcd:0012:0000:0000:0000:0000 -
2001:db8:abcd:0012:ffff:ffff:ffff:ffff

The portion is written in bold marks the network portion of the IP address or prefix. The part written in non-bold is marks the host portion of the address since it will identify the individual host on the network.

IPV6 Addresses

An IPV6 address has 8 groups with numbers. Let us discuss these:

- Network address- these are the first 3 groupings of the address numbers in the subnet mask (first 48 bits).

- Subnet address- this is the fourth grouping of the numbers in the subnet mask (49th to 64th bit).
- Device address- these are the last four groupings of the numbers in the subnet mask (last 64 bits).

Consider the IPV6 address given below:

2001:db8:abcd:0022:0000:0000:0000:0000

In the above example, the network address is **2001:db8:abcd** while the **22** is the subnet address (using short form notation and doing away with zeroes). These two groupings together form an IPV6 *prefix*. The 0000:0000:0000:0000 forms the device address.

Every device on a network has a unique device address. However, the portions for network address and subnet address in an IPV6 address are the same for all network devices. This means that the first four groupings of numbers remain constant in each IPV6 address while the last four groupings keep on varying from device to device. One may simplify the list of devices by substituting the prefix length in place of device address portion of an IPV6 address. This part, that is, the prefix-length is responsible for specifying the range of devices. We express it using a slash (/) followed by an integer ranging between 1 and 128. Consider the prefix /64 specified as shown below:

2001:db8:abcd:0022::/64

The above instructs the system to subdivide the network into a total of 64 subnets. Every subnetwork will have $1/64^{th}$ of the network devices.

Chapter 4

LAN Switching

LAN switching is a type of packet switching in which data packets are transferred from one computer to another over a network. Switching technologies play a vital role in networks as they ensure that packets are sent where they should be sending. LAN switching is good for improving the efficiency of a LAN and ensuring that bandwidth issues are prevented or minimized.

Hierarchical Layered LAN Design Model

The way a LAN is designed plays a great role in determining the efficiency of communications in the LAN. The hierarchical layered model is recommended by Cisco. In this model, you must consider three layers depending on the size of your enterprise:

- Core layer
- Distribution layer
- Access layer.

At the bottom of the model, we have the *access* layer. This is the layer that connects to the end user devices like printers, PCs, IP phones and many other devices.

At the center of the model we have the *distribution* layer. The purpose of this layer is to aggregate data from access layer. It is responsible for controlling traffic in lower levels and prioritizing the traffic based on the organization policies that were implemented during the configuration of switches. Typically, it is expected that this layer should have redundant devices and that its switches should be faster than those used in the access layer.

At the top of the model we have the *core* layer. This layer is responsible for a high speed switching. This is the layer where the fastest switches in the network should be implemented and provides the highest bandwidth since the communication to the other networks from lower levels has to be forwarded through these switches.

This models has a clear definition of roles, hence it is easy to scale the network. Each layer of the LAN has clear security measures that makes the entire LAN secure from security attacks. This means that the data flowing through the network is safe and secure. With this model, we can achieve a higher performance if it is designed well. Also, if the right devices are used, there will be a higher performance. High-speed switches should be used in the core layer of the model to enhance the performance of the model.

The hierarchical LAN design model makes the management of the network an easy process. If there is a need to implement any changes in the network, it becomes easy for the network administrator to do so. The reason is that the role of the devices in each layer is well known.

CSMA/CD

The CSMA/SD stands for *carrier sense multiple access with collision detection.* LAN networks rely on multiple rules to operate. In this communication, the devices on a similar Ethernet segment listen to network media to know whether they are able to transmit or wait. During the early days when hubs were used, only one device could transmit at a time. However, switches allow multiple devices to use the media at once.

Ethernet Communications

There are three ways of sending messages in Ethernet communications. These include:

- Unicast
- Multicast
- Broadcast

In the unicast communication, a frame of data is send from one node to a specified destination. There exists only one sender and one recipient. The sender, the recipient and the switch that are at their center must know each other. This forms the popular way of communication in modern LANs, especially on the internet that uses protocols like Telnet, HTTP and others.

In a multicast communication, the sender is allowed to send a frame to a group of nodes on an Ethernet segment. The type of protocol that is being used can determine whether a multicast is used or not. Suppose you need to do teleconferencing call by communicating to other people at once? This is a good situation for you to send a multicast message.

In some cases, you may need to get a certain type of information not knowing the user who has or knows that information. This is a good situation for you to use a broadcast. In such a case, the frame will be send to every device on the LAN. This communication also becomes important when you have a message that should be received by a large audience. In Ethernet, a physical addressing is used, which is MAC address. This address is used to communicate the frames. After receiving packets from network layer, they are encapsulated to form frames. The encapsulation includes addition of information like the source and destination MAC addresses.

We have stated that the MAC address is the type of address used in Ethernet communications. The address consists of 48 bits represented in hexadecimal format. IP addresses are divided into two segments, that is, the network and host address portion. A MAC address is also divided into two sections:

- Organization Unique Identifier (OUI)
- Vendor assigned number

The first 24 bits of the MAC address forms the OUI. It is a code assigned by IEEE to a certain vendor. The next 24 bits of the MAC address marks the unique number that the vendor has assigned to that device. This number helps to uniquely identify that device.

Duplex Settings in Ethernet

In Ethernet, two modes of communication are used. Duplex determines whether a communication will be unidirectional or bidirectional. The two modes of duplex communications are:

- Half duplex
- Full duplex

In half duplex communication, data is transmitted in one way, meaning that each device is only allowed to send or receive data, not both. This was the kind of communication used during the days of Hubs. A good example of a half-duplex communication is the walkie-talkie with which you can either talk or listen, not both. Due to the nature of this communication, there are high chances of a collision occurring. To prevent or minimize this, CSMA/CD is used. In a full duplex communication, there is a bidirectional flow of data. This means that devices are allowed to send and receive information at the same time. This forms the default mode of communication in modern switches. There are minimal chances of having a collision.

MAC Address Table

Routers must make decisions on where to forward packets, and these decisions are mad based on the routing table. Also, switches have a database in which they keep information. This database has addresses. The database is known as the MAC-Address table and switches rely on it to make decisions regarding forwarding of frames. During communication, switches rely on this information to determine the source and the destination of frames. A switch has to follow the steps given below before forwarding a frame:

1. The switch receives the frame from a port.
2. The switch checks to know whether it has the source port from which the frame was received. If not, the source MAC address of the address is added to the switch's MAC address table.
3. The switch checks to determine it has the destination MAC address for the frame in the MAC address table. If not, the frame is broadcast to all other ports except the port from which the frame was received.
4. Once the destination node has replied, the switch will add the MAC address to its MAC-address table. The subsequent communication to the node will be unicast rather than being broadcast.

Switch Configuration

Switches run an operating system known as IOS (internetworking operating system).

IOS has three command modes namely the user exec mode, privileged exec mode and global configuration mode. Each mode has its own purpose and a number of commands that we can run in that mode. Let us describe these modes:

User EXEC Mode

Initially, the user is logged into this mode. It is the mode that has the least number of commands. To know the list of commands supported in this mode, type?

The commands used in this mode are used for showing statistics and troubleshooting. The prompt shown on left side of the prompt displays the device hostname which is then followed by the > character.

We can abbreviate all commands by using the first letters of their names. For example, *ping* command can be abbreviated to *pin*. The reason is that we don't have any other command in the user exec mode of IOS with same letters.

Privileged EXEC Mode

This mode is also known as *enable* as one has to run the *enable* command to move from user EXEC mode to privileged EXEC mode. This mode also supports more commands compared to the former mode. You can save the configuration of the device or reload it while in this mode. You can get into the third mode, that is, configuration mode from this mode. To access the privileged EXEC mode from user EXEC mode, you must enter a password.

While in the privileged EXEC mode, a # is shown after the hostname.

Global Configuration Mode

The configuration of a device is changed in the global configuration mode. To get into this mode, you must type *configure terminal (or config t in short form)* while in enable mode. In this mode, the prompt shows *hostname* (config).

The commands for this mode are good for device configuration. You can use them to configure device hostname, set IP address for interface, configure authentication etc. You can access sub modes while in this mode. For example, the interface mode is where you can configure an interface.

To get back to privileged EXEC mode, you type *end* command. You can also press CTRL + C to exit the configuration mode.

Hostnames, console & vty lines, banners and passwords

These essential are for each switch. You can create a physical lab or a topology in packet tracer with the devices that you want. I will be showing you how to configure a switch using the console cable. The setup should be as shown below:

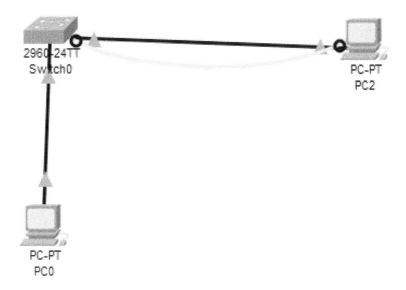

The non-black connection between the switch0 and PC2 is a console cable connected to console port of the switch and the RS32 port of PC2. The black connections are copper straight through cables.

We now need to configure the switch. Click it and choose CLI. Press enter key. You will be taken to the user EXEC mode symbolized by the > symbol:

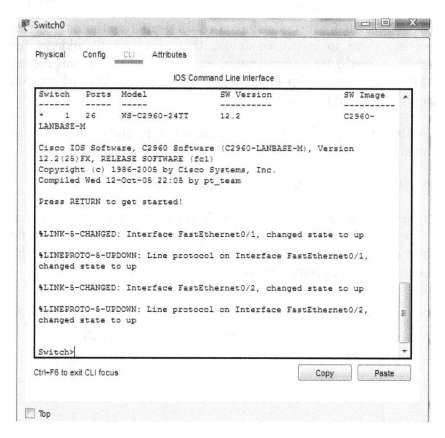

Remember that6 configuration of a switch should be done in the global configuration mode. Let us first get to the privileged EXEC mode by typing *enable* command:

enable

We can then get to the global configuration mode by typing *config t*:

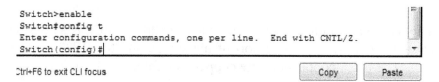

We are now in the global configuration mode of the switch and we can perform the necessary configuration.

Our first configuration is to change the hostname of the switch from the default to *SWITCH_1*. This can be done by running this command:

hostname SWITCH_1

After running the above command, you realize that the terminal will change the value before the prompt, that is, #, to the name assigned to the switch:

```
Switch(config)#hostname SWITCH_1
SWITCH_1(config)#
```

This shows that the host has been renamed successfully.

We now need to configure line console and 5 telnet line options like password, logging synchronous and executive timeouts. Let us configure the passwords to *password* and the timeout to 15 minutes:

line console 0
password password
login
logging synchronous
exec-timeout 15 0
exit

```
SWITCH_1(config)#line console 0
SWITCH_1(config-line)#password password
SWITCH_1(config-line)#login
SWITCH_1(config-line)#logging synchronous
SWITCH_1(config-line)#exec-timeout 15 0
SWITCH_1(config-line)#exit
SWITCH_1(config)#
```

We have successfully configured the line console. Let us now configure the 5 telnet line options:

line vty 0 4
password password
login

logging synchronous
exec-timeout 15 0
exit

```
SWITCH_1(config)#line vty 0 4
SWITCH_1(config-line)#password password
SWITCH_1(config-line)#login
SWITCH_1(config-line)#logging synchronous
SWITCH_1(config-line)#exec-time-out 15 0
                                 ^
% Invalid input detected at '^' marker.

SWITCH_1(config-line)#exec-timeout 15 0
SWITCH_1(config-line)#exit
SWITCH_1(config)#|
```

The *login synchronous* command prevents unnecessary messages from appearing on the screen while typing hence disrupting the command as it is typed.

After configuring the passwords, you have noticed that we ran the *login* command. This command tells the IOS to prompt the user to enter that password when they attempting to log into the switch. There are a number of reasons why an administrator may need to display such a message, for example, to warn users of unauthorized access to the switch.

To configure the banner, we use the *Banner MOTD* command with the following syntax:

Banner MOTD #<message>#

The MOTD stands for M*essage Of The Day*. The beginning and the end of the message is marked using the pound symbol (#).

We want to set the banner message to "WARNING, AUTHORIZED ACCESS ONLY!!!"To set this, we run the following command:

banner motd # WARNING, AUTHORIZED ACCESS ONLY!!!#

```
User Access Verification

Password:

SWITCH_1>enable
SWITCH_1#config t
Enter configuration commands, one per line.  End with CNTL/Z.
SWITCH_1(config)#banner motd # WARNING, AUTHORIZED ACCESS ONLY!!!#
SWITCH_1(config)#
```

The banner has been set successfully.

If you need to access a router from a remote location via the vty lines, you use an IP address. For the case of switches, an IP address should be configured a subnet mask and default gateway where the IP address is used for management of the switch. If you are using switching a CISCO switch, the vlan1 is set as the default management VLAN. However, it is recommended that you change this for management purposes.

For us to enable management of a switch via management interface, we should create a management VLAN then assign to it a management IP address. Let us use the VLAN 99 and assign it an IP address of 192.168.99.1. This will allow for management of the switch remotely via vty lines.

We also need to configure a default gateway so that the traffic for remote networks may be accessed through the switch. Let us set the default gateway to an IP address of 192.168.1.1. The following steps will help us configure the management interface. We will use the *interface vlan* command to help us configure a switched virtual interface (SVI).We should first create the management interface, which is VLAN 99:

interface vlan 99

We can then assign it an IP address and a subnet mask. We should then activate it via the *no shutdown* command:

ip address 192.168.99.1 255.255.255.0
no shutdown
exit

```
SWITCH_1(config)#interface vlan 99
SWITCH_1(config-if)#ip address 192.168.99.1 255.255.255.0
SWITCH_1(config-if)#no shutdown
SWITCH_1(config-if)#exit
SWITCH_1(config)#
```

We need to link one of the interfaces on the router to the VLAN 99, which is the management VLAN. For now just note the command but we will discuss them later:

int fa0/5
switchport mode access
switchport access vlan 99
end
copy running-config startup-config

```
SWITCH_1(config)#int fa0/5
SWITCH_1(config-if)#switchport mode access
SWITCH_1(config-if)#switchport access vlan 99
% Access VLAN does not exist. Creating vlan 99
SWITCH_1(config-if)#
%LINK-5-CHANGED: Interface Vlan99, changed state to up

SWITCH_1(config-if)#end
SWITCH_1#
%SYS-5-CONFIG_I: Configured from console by console

SWITCH_1#copy running-config startup-config
Destination filename [startup-config]?
Building configuration...
[OK]
SWITCH_1#
```

We started with the *int* command which stands for *interface*. You can also write it in full instead of abbreviating it.

Consider the last command used above:

copy running-config startup-config

The command simply helps us to save the changes that we have made to the device.

We now need to configure the ip default gateway for forwarding of traffic destined to remote networks. This can be done by running the command IP DEFAULT-GATEWAY <IP ADDRESS>.

Let us run the following command using the IP address of 192.168.1.1:

ip default-gateway 192.168.1.1

Once you are done with the above configuration, all the devices on the network should be capable of communicating with no additional configuration.

If you had not configured the IP addresses for the PCs, you can still do it. Click the PC0 and go to Desktop tab then choose "IP Configuration". Do the configuration from there. Assign PC0 an IP address of 192.168.1.2 and a default gateway of 192.168.1.1. Assign PC2 an IP address of 192.168.1.3 and a default gateway of 192.168.1.1. The subnet mask in all should be 255.255.255.0.

You can then ping PC2 from PC0 by clicking PC0, choosing Desktop tab then "Command Prompt". Run the *ping* command as shown below:

ping 192.168.1.3

```
Packet Tracer PC Command Line 1.0
C:\>ping 192.168.1.3

Pinging 192.168.1.3 with 32 bytes of data:

Reply from 192.168.1.3: bytes=32 time=91ms TTL=128
Reply from 192.168.1.3: bytes=32 time<1ms TTL=128
Reply from 192.168.1.3: bytes=32 time<1ms TTL=128
Reply from 192.168.1.3: bytes=32 time<1ms TTL=128

Ping statistics for 192.168.1.3:
    Packets: Sent = 4, Received = 4, Lost = 0 (0% loss),
Approximate round trip times in milli-seconds:
    Minimum = 0ms, Maximum = 91ms, Average = 22ms

C:\>
```

The two PCs are able to communicate. The pinged PC send echo replies messages.

Duplex Settings

The purpose of duplex settings is to determine whether communication will be unidirectional or bidirectional. CISCO switches come with a default setting of auto for this. This means you have one side operating in half-duplex, the port will also be half-duplex. We can hard code the switch ports to operate in full duplex since it is the most recommended mode of communication. The command should be executed in interface configuration mode. Remember what we did in previous case, we used the *int*/interface command. This command takes us to the interface configuration mode. Let us change the fast Ethernet 0/1 on the switch to full duplex mode:

interface fa0/1

duplex full

```
SWITCH_1(config-if)#interface fa0/1
SWITCH_1(config-if)#duplex full
SWITCH_1(config-if)#
%LINK-3-UPDOWN: Interface FastEthernet0/1, changed state to down

%LINEPROTO-5-UPDOWN: Line protocol on Interface FastEthernet0/1,
changed state to down

SWITCH 1(config-if)#
```

Port Security

Switches are vulnerable to many security n breaches. Let us discuss some of the attacks that switches are prone to:

- MAC addresses spoofing- this occurs when an attacker gains unauthorized access into a switch via a node. They use a tool to send source MAC addresses that are invalid to the switch. The operation of switches relies on a MAC address table. This table can only take a certain number of MAC addresses. When this table becomes filled, the switch is unable to forward traffic via a unicast, making it behave like a hub by flooding frames out of all ports. The attacker will be able to see all frames originating from all network nodes.

- MAC-address spoofing- in this type of attacker, the attacker poses as if he is a DHCP (Domain Host Configuration Protocol) server. When the legitimate clients request to be provided with an IP address from the DHCP server, the attacker assigns them an IP address that they will be able to see traffic from a certain host.

Employing port security is one of the ways that an administrator can ensure that the switch is secured from such attacks. All interfaces or ports on the switch should be secured before the switch is deployed into a production environment. With port security, we can limit the number of valid MAC addresses that are allowed on a port. Here are some of the port configuration options that can help you achieve port security:

1. Using statically configured MAC addresses. This involves assigning every port on the switch to a specific node by hard coding the MAC address of that node to that port. Only devices that match the MAC address configuration of that port will be able to connect to it. However, for that case of a large network, configuring this might be a nightmare.
2. Dynamic secure MAC addresses. This involves configuring the switch ports to learn and store the MAC address of user devices.
3. Using sticky MAC addresses. This will help ensure that only the MAC addresses that are learnt dynamically are able to use the switch. The addresses are in turn saved in the running configuration file of the switch. When the switch is rebooted, they will be lost.
4. It is possible for us to configure the maximum number of MAC addresses that should be allowed to access any particular switch port. This will help us prevent MAC address spoofing.

Security Violations

Security violations determine the kind of action to be taken if a certain access to a port doesn't meet some specified requirements or specifications. The violation is detected through the security mechanism that you implement on the switch.

Here are some of the violations that such events can trigger:

1. Protect- in this mechanism, the switch will drop the frames that originate from the node that breaches the security without notifying the administrator that a breach has occurred.
2. Restrict- if one of the security policies is violated, the switch will drop the frames from that port then record the breach. In majority of the cases, this involves sending an SNMP trap, increasing the violation counter then sending a syslog message.
3. Shutdown- after detection of a security violation, the port on which the frames were received is shutdown. The switch will also send a message to the administrator using syslog and SNMP. The violation counter will also record the breach. The administrator is the only one allowed to reactivate the port once they have investigated the breach.

Suppose we have the following setup:

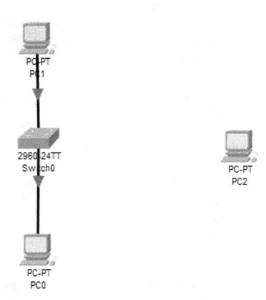

PC1 is connected to0 fa0/1 interface of the switch. PC0 is connected to fa0/2 interface of the switch. We want to set the security violation of PC0 to strict.

The port that has been connected to PC1 will be set to a violation mode of strict. The fa0/3 port of the switch will be set to a violation mode of shutdown. The security of the ports can be configured by going through the steps given below:

The fa0/1 interface of the switch has been connected to PC1. Let us configure it:

First, let us get to the interface configuration mode:

interface fa0/1

Let us enable the port security by running the following commands then enable protect violation mode of the switch:

switchport port security

switchport port-security violation protect

```
Switch(config-if)#interface fa0/1
Switch(config-if)#switchport port-security
Command rejected: FastEthernet0/1 is a dynamic port.
Switch(config-if)#switchport port-security violation protect
Switch(config-if)#
```

We can now bind the Mac address of PC1 to port fa0/1 of the switch. This will mean that in case any other node connects to the port, the switch will not allow it to transmit. We can do this by configuring the port with a MAC address of the PC. Just run the following command:

switchport port-security mac-address <MAC Address>

The NIC (Network Interface Card) of the PC comes with the MAC address of the PC.

The final step should be to define the maximum number of MAC addresses that are allowed to access the port. In our case, we need to allow only one MAC address such that if any other device tries to access the port, it will be protected.

Run this command:

switchport port-security maximum
<MAXIMUM_NUMBER_OF_MAC_ADDRESSES>

In this case, we should set it to 1, so that command should be as follows:

switchport port-security maximum 1

Now that you have made the above configurations, you can save them to the NVRAM (NVRAM). This means that you run the previous command, that is:

copy running-config startup-config

To configure the security violations of restrict and shutdown, we run the following commands:

switchport port-security violation <restrict>

switchport port-security violation <shutdown>

It is also possible for us to configure the type of MAC addresses that we need to access the switch ports. The use of a static mac address is good but it can be a challenge if there are thousands of mac addresses in the network. In such a case, we can use sticky mac addresses, meaning that once a node is connected to a switchport, its mac address will be learnt and stored in the memory of the switch. The following command can help you configure a sticky mac address:

switchport port-security mac-address sticky

It is recommended that you should configure the maximum number of mac addresses on the port so that other people don' use their devices on the port. To see the port security configuration of a port, use the following command:

show port-security <interface-number>

There exists several commands that can be used for verification of operation of switches and troubleshoot when issues arise. Let us discuss these commands:

show running-config - this command returns the current configuration of the switch. Here is a section of the output from the command:

```
Switch#show running-config
Building configuration...

Current configuration : 1124 bytes
!
version 12.2
no service timestamps log datetime msec
no service timestamps debug datetime msec
no service password-encryption
!
hostname Switch
!
!
!
!
!
spanning-tree mode pvst
spanning-tree extend system-id
!
interface FastEthernet0/1
 switchport port-security violation restrict
!
```

The command helps you to see the configurations that have been made on the switch.

show mac-address-table - this command should return all the mac addresses that the switch is aware of. It is a good command when you need to know whether there are nodes on the switchports.

show interface <name & number> switchport - this command returns various switchport statistics. For example

show interface fa0/1 switchport

```
Switch#show interface fa0/1 switchport
Name: Fa0/1
Switchport: Enabled
Administrative Mode: dynamic auto
Operational Mode: down
Administrative Trunking Encapsulation: dot1q
Operational Trunking Encapsulation: native
Negotiation of Trunking: On
Access Mode VLAN: 1 (default)
Trunking Native Mode VLAN: 1 (default)
Voice VLAN: none
Administrative private-vlan host-association: none
Administrative private-vlan mapping: none
Administrative private-vlan trunk native VLAN: none
Administrative private-vlan trunk encapsulation: dot1q
Administrative private-vlan trunk normal VLANs: none
Administrative private-vlan trunk private VLANs: none
Operational private-vlan: none
Trunking VLANs Enabled: All
Pruning VLANs Enabled: 2-1001
Capture Mode Disabled
Capture VLANs Allowed: ALL
Protected: false
Unknown unicast blocked: disabled
```

Chapter 5

*V*LANs

VLANs refers to a way of dividing a switch into various LAN segments. All networks that are connected to a switch are 1 broadcast domain. This is an indication that all devices that are connected to a switch use one IP subnet by default.

VLANs provide us with a way of dividing a switch into smaller broadcast domains making it possible for us to implement many subnets in only one switch. This means a VLAN is simply a way of creating multiple logical switches on your physical switch. Every logical switch will use its own IP subnet.

Why use VLANs?

VLANs are very important to the networks of today. Here are the reasons as to why they are important:

1. Security- with VLANs, it is possible for us to use a single physical device for users having different access rights. Traffic coming from a sensitive group can use a similar switch as that of a group with a common traffic without necessarily violating security policies.
2. Reduced costs- when using VLANs, the costs that could have been incurred when using physical switches in each department are reduced. With VLANs, users in different departments can be separated without acquiring new hardware.
3. Improved performance- as stated earlier, the default operation of a switch is in one broadcast domain. This means if a frame is destined to a node whose mac address is not in the mac address table, the switch will first broadcast it to all switch ports. This can lead to a degraded network performance. When using VLANs, the broadcast is usually limited to a certain VLAN.
4. Improved Administrative Tasks- when VLANs are configured, the work that network administrators must do to manage the network is reduced. Tasks such as upgrading the network, troubleshooting and others are made simple.

Trunks

When we are using VLANs on numerous switches, the interconnection between switches is referred to as a *trunk*. A trunk can be seen as a highway connecting numerous small roads. The work of the trunk is to allow traffic coming from many VLANs to move between switches.

If you are using a CISCO switch, you can allow configuring any of the two trunks namely *ISL trunk* and *IEEE 802.1Q* trunk ports.

The following concepts are important and you should note them whenever you are configuring a trunk:

Native VLAN

This marks the port to be used by the switch for sending any untagged traffic. Tagged traffic refers to all traffic that is destined to a certain VLAN. Untagged traffic refers to any traffic that is not destined to any certain VLAN like control information.

Dynamic Trunk Protocol

This is a CISCO proprietary protocol responsible for negotiating the trunking modes between the switches. The cisco switch ports can operate in any of the following three modes:

- Access
- Trunk
- Dynamic

An access port refers to a port connecting to an end device like an IP phone or a computer.

A trunk port refers to a port carrying both tagged and untagged traffic across switches and in some cases a router.

The work of a DTP (Dynamic Trunk Protocol) is to negotiate the port's operation mode in a CISCO switch. If one of the ends has been configured as a trunk, DTP will determine the mode to be used for operation on the other end of connection.

Creating VLANs

You now know the various basics of VLANs. You also appreciate the benefits that are associated with the creation and use of VLANs. We now need to demonstrate how to create VLANs. Create the topology given below:

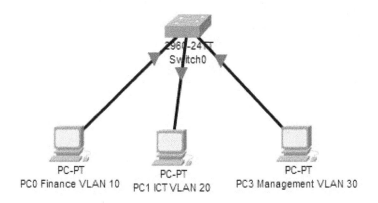

PCO in VLAN 10 is connected to fa0/1 interface on the switch, PC1 on VLAN 20 to fa0/2 of the switch and PC3 on VLAN 30 connected to fa0/3 interface on the switch. Let us do the basic configuration on the switch:

Switch>enable
Switch#config t
Enter configuration commands, one per line. End with CNTL/Z.
Switch(config)#hostname SWITCH_A
SWITCH_A(config)#line con 0
SWITCH_A(config-line)#password password
SWITCH_A(config-line)#login
SWITCH_A(config-line)#logging synchronous
SWITCH_A(config-line)#exec-timeout 30 0
SWITCH_A(config-line)#exit
SWITCH_A(config)#line vty 0 4
SWITCH_A(config-line)#password password
SWITCH_A(config-line)#login
SWITCH_A(config-line)#logging synchronous

SWITCH_A(config-line)#exec-timeou 30 0
SWITCH_A(config-line)#exit
SWITCH_A(config)#

```
Switch>enable
Switch#config t
Enter configuration commands, one per line.  End with CNTL/Z.
Switch(config)#hostname SWITCH_A
SWITCH_A(config)#line con 0
SWITCH_A(config-line)#password password
SWITCH_A(config-line)#login
SWITCH_A(config-line)#logging synchronous
SWITCH_A(config-line)#exec-timeout 30 0
SWITCH_A(config-line)#exit
SWITCH_A(config)#line vty 0 4
SWITCH_A(config-line)#password password
SWITCH_A(config-line)#login
SWITCH_A(config-line)#logging synchronous
SWITCH_A(config-line)#exec-timeou 30 0
SWITCH_A(config-line)#exit
SWITCH_A(config)#
```

We can now get into configuring the VLANs. In our case, we have three VLANs as shown below:

- VLAN 10- Finance
- VLAN 20- ICT
- VLAN 30- Management

To configure the VLANs, you must open the switch and get into the global configuration mode. You can then use the following command in that mode:

vlan <VLAN_NUMBER>

The VLAN_NUMBER should be a unique number ranging between 1 and 1005. However, there exist some preserved VLANs. After running the above command, you will be taken to VLAN configuration mode. It is in that mode that we can name the modes in the way we named them in the diagram. The configuration of the three VLANs can be done by running the following commands:

SWITCH_A(config)#vlan 10
SWITCH_A(config-vlan)#name FINANCE

SWITCH_A(config-vlan)#exit
SWITCH_A(config)#vlan 20
SWITCH_A(config-vlan)#name ICT
SWITCH_A(config-vlan)#exit
SWITCH_A(config)#vlan 30
SWITCH_A(config-vlan)#name MANAGEMENT
SWITCH_A(config-vlan)#exit
SWITCH_A(config)#

```
SWITCH_A(config)#vlan 10
SWITCH_A(config-vlan)#name FINANCE
SWITCH_A(config-vlan)#exit
SWITCH_A(config)#vlan 20
SWITCH_A(config-vlan)#name ICT
SWITCH_A(config-vlan)#exit
SWITCH_A(config)#vlan 30
SWITCH_A(config-vlan)#name MANAGEMENT
SWITCH_A(config-vlan)#exit
SWITCH_A(config)#
```

Assigning Ports to VLANs

It is now time for us to assign ports to the VLANs we have just configured. This should again be done in the interface configuration mode.

PC0 has been connected to fa0/1 interface of the switch. The port configuration can be done by running the following commands:

SWITCH_A(config)#interface fa0/1
SWITCH_A(config-if)#switchport mode access
SWITCH_A(config-if)#switchport access vlan 10
SWITCH_A(config-if)#

```
SWITCH_A(config)#interface fa0/1
SWITCH_A(config-if)#switchport mode access
SWITCH_A(config-if)#switchport access vlan 10
SWITCH_A(config-if)#
```

Notice that we ran the *switchport mode access* command. This means that this port is an access port and it can only support traffic that is coming from one VLAN. The second command was *switchport access vlan 10*. This means that the node that is connected to this port is only allowed to access VLAN 10. This means that the ip subnet for the port should be the same for all the nodes on VLAN 10.

Here are the commands needed for assigning switchports connected to the other PCs to their VLANs:

SWITCH_A(config)#interface fa0/2
SWITCH_A(config-if)#switchport mode access
SWITCH_A(config-if)#switchport access vlan 20
SWITCH_A(config-if)#exit
SWITCH_A(config)#interface fa0/3
SWITCH_A(config-if)#switchport mode access
SWITCH_A(config-if)#switchport access vlan 30
SWITCH_A(config-if)#exit
SWITCH_A(config)#

```
SWITCH_A(config)#interface fa0/2
SWITCH_A(config-if)#switchport mode access
SWITCH_A(config-if)#switchport access vlan 20
SWITCH_A(config-if)#exit
SWITCH_A(config)#interface fa0/3
SWITCH_A(config-if)#switchport mode access
SWITCH_A(config-if)#switchport access vlan 30
SWITCH_A(config-if)#exit
SWITCH_A(config)#
```

Configuring Port Security

Now that we have assigned the VLANs to their respective ports, we can go ahead and configure the ports for security. We need to configure all the three ports, setting a maximum of 1 mac address per port and set the security violation mode to shutdown. Let us run the following commands:

SWITCH_A(config)#int fa0/1

```
SWITCH_A(config-if)#switchport port-security
SWITCH_A(config-if)#switchport port-security maximum 1
SWITCH_A(config-if)#switchport port-security violation
shutdown
SWITCH_A(config-if)#switchport port-security mac-address
sticky
SWITCH_A(config-if)#exit
SWITCH_A(config)#int fa0/2
SWITCH_A(config-if)#switchport port-security
SWITCH_A(config-if)#switchport port-security maximum 1
SWITCH_A(config-if)#switchport port-security violation
shutdown
SWITCH_A(config-if)#switchport port-security mac-address
sticky
SWITCH_A(config-if)#exit
SWITCH_A(config)#int fa0/3
SWITCH_A(config-if)#switchport port-security
SWITCH_A(config-if)#switchport port-security maximum 1
SWITCH_A(config-if)#switchport port-security violation
shutdown
SWITCH_A(config-if)#switchport port-security mac-address
sticky
SWITCH_A(config-if)#exit
SWITCH_A(config)#
```

```
SWITCH_A(config)#int fa0/1
SWITCH_A(config-if)#switchport port-security
SWITCH_A(config-if)#switchport port-security maximum 1
SWITCH_A(config-if)#switchport port-security violation shutdown
SWITCH_A(config-if)#switchport port-security mac-address sticky
SWITCH_A(config-if)#exit
SWITCH_A(config)#int fa0/2
SWITCH_A(config-if)#switchport port-security
SWITCH_A(config-if)#switchport port-security maximum 1
SWITCH_A(config-if)#switchport port-security violation shutdown
SWITCH_A(config-if)#switchport port-security mac-address sticky
SWITCH_A(config-if)#exit
SWITCH_A(config)#int fa0/3
SWITCH_A(config-if)#switchport port-security
SWITCH_A(config-if)#switchport port-security maximum 1
SWITCH_A(config-if)#switchport port-security violation shutdown
SWITCH_A(config-if)#switchport port-security mac-address sticky
SWITCH_A(config-if)#exit
SWITCH_A(config)#
```

Configuring the Trunk Port

We now need to configure the trunk port on the switch which should be fa0/5. This can be done by running these commands:

SWITCH_A(config)#int fa0/5
SWITCH_A(config-if)#switchport mode trunk
SWITCH_A(config-if)#switchport trunk native vlan 1
SWITCH_A(config-if)#exit
SWITCH_A(config)#

```
SWITCH_A(config)#int fa0/5
SWITCH_A(config-if)#switchport mode trunk
SWITCH_A(config-if)#switchport trunk native vlan 1
SWITCH_A(config-if)#exit
SWITCH_A(config)#
```

Notice the use of the following command:

switchport trunk native vlan 1

The command simply specifies that the native VLAN on the switch is VLAN 1. It is recommended that you configure the native VLAN using some other ID other than the default one which is VLAN 1.

Deleting VLANs

When you add "no" at the beginning of a command, you negate what the command does.

Unlike other commands, the VLANs that you create are not kept in startup configuration. If you execute the *"show running-config"* command on your switches, you will realize that the switches that you have configured won't show up. The reason is that VLANs are not stored in the running config but in a file named *VLAN.dat.*

If you have configured one of the VLANs, you can delete it by running the following command:

no vlan <VLAN_ID>

However, if you need to delete all VLANs, you can get to the privileged EXEC mode of the switch and run the following command:

delete flash:vlan.dat

Verifying VLANs Configuration

To verify whether the VLANs that we have configured have taken effect and are operating in the correct ports, you can run the command given below in the privileged exec mode of the witch:

show vlan brief

The command returns the following in our switch:

The output shows that there are a total of 8 VLANs in the switch, with the default VLAN having an ID of 1. The three VLANs that we configured, that is, VLAN 10, 20 and 30 were created and they are now active. Their respective interfaces on the switch are also shown. The VLANs 1, 1003, 1004, and 1005 are kept on by default. The VLANs 1003 - 1005 can't be changed as they are reserved.

```
SWITCH_A#show vlan brief

VLAN Name                             Status    Ports
---- -------------------------------- ---------
--------------------------------
1    default                          active    Fa0/4, Fa0/5, Fa0/6,
Fa0/7
                                                Fa0/8, Fa0/9, Fa0/10,
Fa0/11
                                                Fa0/12, Fa0/13,
Fa0/14, Fa0/15
                                                Fa0/16, Fa0/17,
Fa0/18, Fa0/19
                                                Fa0/20, Fa0/21,
Fa0/22, Fa0/23
                                                Fa0/24, Gig0/1,
Gig0/2
10   FINANCE                          active    Fa0/1
20   ICT                              active    Fa0/2
30   MANAGEMENT                       active    Fa0/3
1002 fddi-default                     active
1003 token-ring-default               active
1004 fddinet-default                  active
1005 trnet-default                    active
SWITCH A#
```

Consider the following command:

show interface <interface_id> switchport

The command can be used for verifying the operational status and the VLAN that has been configured on an interface. To show this for the interface fast Ethernet 0/1, you can run the following command:

show int fa0/1 switchport

The command returns the following in my case:

```
SWITCH_A#show int fa0/1 switchport
Name: Fa0/1
Switchport: Enabled
Administrative Mode: static access
Operational Mode: down
Administrative Trunking Encapsulation: dot1q
Operational Trunking Encapsulation: native
Negotiation of Trunking: Off
Access Mode VLAN: 10 (FINANCE)
Trunking Native Mode VLAN: 1 (default)
Voice VLAN: none
Administrative private-vlan host-association: none
Administrative private-vlan mapping: none
Administrative private-vlan trunk native VLAN: none
Administrative private-vlan trunk encapsulation: dot1q
Administrative private-vlan trunk normal VLANs: none
Administrative private-vlan trunk private VLANs: none
Operational private-vlan: none
Trunking VLANs Enabled: All
Pruning VLANs Enabled: 2-1001
Capture Mode Disabled
Capture VLANs Allowed: ALL
Protected: false
Unknown unicast blocked: disabled
Unknown multicast blocked: disabled
Appliance trust: none


SWITCH_A#
```

From the above output, you can see that the switchport mode has been set to static access. This is an indication that the port has been configured so as to operate in access mode. VLAN 10 is shown as the configured VLAN. The port is unable to negotiate a trunk link since you can see the line for "Negotiation of Trunking: Off".

To see the details of a specific VLAN, you can use either of these commands:

show vlan <name> <vlan_name>
show vlan <id> <vlan_ID>

Let us explore the details of the ICT VLAN:

show vlan name ICT

This returns the following:

```
SWITCH_A#show vlan name ICT

VLAN Name                             Status    Ports
---- -------------------------------- --------- -------------------------------
20   ICT                              active    Fa0/2

VLAN Type  SAID       MTU   Parent RingNo BridgeNo Stp  BrdgMode Trans1 Trans2
---- ----- ---------- ----- ------ ------ -------- ---- -------- ------ ------
20   enet  100020     1500  -      -      -        -    -        0      0

SWITCH_A#
```

The output clearly shows that the VLAN named ICT has only 1 switch port, that is, fa0/2. To use the VLAN ID, we can run the following command;

show vlan id 10

This returns the details of the FINANCE VLAN as shown below:

```
SWITCH_A#show vlan id 10

VLAN Name                             Status    Ports
---- -------------------------------- --------- -------------------------------
10   FINANCE                          active    Fa0/1

VLAN Type  SAID       MTU   Parent RingNo BridgeNo Stp  BrdgMode Trans1 Trans2
---- ----- ---------- ----- ------ ------ -------- ---- -------- ------ ------
10   enet  100010     1500  -      -      -        -    -        0      0

SWITCH A#
```

The *show vlan brief* command can return the details of the various VLANs. It is a good command for troubleshooting purposes:

```
SWITCH_A#show vlan brief

VLAN Name                             Status    Ports
---- -------------------------------- --------- -------------------------------
1    default                          active    Fa0/4, Fa0/5, Fa0/6, Fa0/7
                                                Fa0/8, Fa0/9, Fa0/10, Fa0/11
                                                Fa0/12, Fa0/13, Fa0/14, Fa0/15
                                                Fa0/16, Fa0/17, Fa0/18, Fa0/19
                                                Fa0/20, Fa0/21, Fa0/22, Fa0/23
                                                Fa0/24, Gig0/1, Gig0/2
10   FINANCE                          active    Fa0/1
20   ICT                              active    Fa0/2
30   MANAGEMENT                       active    Fa0/3
1002 fddi-default                     active
1003 token-ring-default               active
1004 fddinet-default                  active
1005 trnet-default                    active
SWITCH A#
```

Chapter 6

Spanning Tree Protocol

We previously discussed the hierarchical network model that is recommended when creating a LAN. It makes it easy for us to assign roles and functions to the various network devices. We also stated that redundancy can be achieved at the core and distribution layers of the model.

In networking, the reason behind implementing redundancy is to keep the users connected even when a major failure occurs on the network. If for example there are redundant paths and one of the paths fail, the traffic will take the alternative path to reach the destination.

Layer 2 Loops

Redundancy is of great importance in the hierarchical network model, but it can lead to loops. You already that switch a mac address table in which they keep the mac addresses of devices that they learn. When two switches are connected tom each other and they exchange data frames with each other, loops may occur.

One of the switches may end up concluding that a PC is directly connected to the other switch when it is in fact connected directly to it. Due to this, the data frames may keep on going round the two switches. Packets have the TTL (Time To Live) field unlike frames. This means that the cycling of the frames between the two switches may continue forever resulting into a loop.

If this happens in a large network, it may lead to a disaster and make the switch to behave like a HUB. The reason is that the MAC address table of the switch will get filled up and the switch will only be able to broadcast traffic.

Broadcast Storms

A broadcast storm is simply what we have discussed in the previous section. It occurs when there is too much broadcast traffic resulting from the occurrence of layer 2 loops.

The effect of this is that all the bandwidth available on the switch will be consumed as the data available will not be forwarded by the switch. Broadcast storms result from loops occurring in the network. If a loop happens at layer 2, it cannot be stopped since a frame doesn't have a field that tells it the time it will age out. This is why there should be backup paths in a LAN and mechanisms for dealing with loops in case they occur.

From the above, you have seen the need for redundancy in a network to handle failures of network points. However, when redundancy is implemented, there are high chances of having a layer 2 loop. The spanning tree protocol helps us solve the problem of loops in switched networks.

How does STP work? It operates by blocking the alternative paths leading to networks and allowing the use of only one path. In case the main path becomes disabled, the STP will reactivate the redundant paths so that communication may continue.

Spanning Tree Algorithm

STP uses the spanning tree algorithm to activate the backup paths in the case of a failure almost instantaneously. Just like the other routing protocols used for networking, the spanning tree algorithm will do a calculation to determine the best paths in a LAN network then block the alternative paths.

Root Bridge

In your LAN network, the spanning tree algorithm will elect one of the switches where all calculations will be done. This is known as the *root bridge*. The switch will ensure there is a correct STP operation.

Root Ports

The STP relies on the root ports for the purpose of forwarding frames. All ports that connect to the root bridge on the neigh boring switches are referred to as *root ports*. Once STP has converged, these ports will always stay in a forwarding state unless a failure occurs.

Designated ports

The ports on root bridges and one port on other links that are not connected directly to the root bridge are referred to as the *designated ports*. STP also uses these ports for the purpose of forwarding frames.

Non-designated ports

One STP has converged fully; some of its ports get blocked, which are redundant ports. These are the non-designated ports in STP and they only become active once a failure has occurred.

Electing the Root Bridge

The root bridge forms the root point in STP and where calculations are done. The root bridge may be any switch on the network that has won the election. The election of the root bridge is determined by BID (bridge ID). This is a field obtained by combining the MAC address of a switch and its priority. Once the root bridge has been elected, the spanning tree algorithm will choose the best paths depending on bandwidths on links or cost. STP assigns different costs to different speed links as shown below:

- 10Gbps- 2
- 1Gbps-4
- 100Mbps- 19
- 10Mbps- 100

Note that the field can be changed with the intention of influencing the path that is chosen as the best path. Note that in the above costs, the lower values are given priority in SPA. This is not the case with other algorithms like OSPF. To understand the STP algorithm, you must know how the election of the root bridge is done. The switches taking part in the election must send a hello message known as *Bridge Protocol Data Unit (BPDU)*. The BPDU has the information described below:

- Root – ID - the MAC address of the switch and its corresponding STP Priority.

- Bridge-ID- the MAC address of root bridge
- Link cost – the STP cost.

Suppose we have the following devices setup:

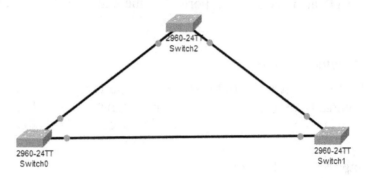

After the boot up of the switches, both the Root ID and BID are identical for all switches on the network. The switches broadcast the BPDU message with this information to the rest of the switches. The intention of the switches is to find the one with lowest BPDU and mark it as designated.

Assume that Switch0 has the lowest MAC address of the three. When the other switches receive the information, they will examine it against their own information with an intention of finding the root bridge. When Switch1 and Switch2 receive the message from Switch0, they will identify Switch0 as the root bridge as it has the lowest Mac address and priority.

Once Switch0 receives this message, it will mark itself as the root bridge since it has the lowest MAC address and priority.

The spanning tree algorithm will then mark all the ports that lead to Switch0 from the other switches as root ports and all ports on Switch0 as designated ports.

The next step involves determining the port that is blocked between Switch1 and Switch2. In that case, the spanning tree algorithm will find the port offering the lowest BPDU between these two switches. The priority will play a great role in determining this and one of the ports will be marked as designated (the one on switch with lowest priority) while the other one will be blocked.

Spanning Tree States and Timers

Now that you have known the various states that ports are marked after election. During the election state, the ports change from one state to another while using three timers. Let us discuss the various states available in STP:

1. Blocking state- any root or non-designated port is considered to be a port in a blocking state. This is a port that isn't forwarding frames. A port in this state will only receive BPDU frames so that it may know the location of the root bridge and know in case a topology change happens.
2. Listening- in the listening state, STP is aware the port is capable of receiving and sending frames. Ports in this state are able to send and receive BPDU frames to notify the neighboring switches that it may be an active port in STP.
3. Learning- this describes a state in which a port is preparing to forward frames. A switch with ports in this state is populating its Mac address table.
4. Forwarding- when a port is active in sending and receiving frames in a network, it is said to be in a forwarding state. The port may also send and receive BPDE frames to check whether any topological changes have been done.
5. Disabled- if a port is in a shutdown mode as a result of configuration by the administrator, it assumes a disabled state.

STP relies on three timers. These timers are responsible for determining the state of a switch or port in STP topology. These timers include the following:

- The Hello timer –this is transmitted after every 2 seconds by default.
- The Forward delay – this is transmitted 15 seconds before transitioning to the forwarding state by default.
- Maximum age –this is transmitted after every 20 seconds by default.

The hello timer message is used to determine if a message is still alive or not. Each port in the topology receives a BPDU frame after each 2 seconds.

This is used as a keep-alive mechanism for determining whether a port in the STO topology is active. However, if you don't like the 2 seconds, the value can be modified to another value that is between 1 and 10 seconds.

The forward delay marks the duration a switch spends in the listening and learning states. In CISCO switches, this value takes a default of 15 seconds for every state but the administrator is allowed to tune it to a value that is between 4 and 30 seconds.

The *ma age time* denotes the maximum length of time a witch port is allowed to save BPDU information. This time has a value of 20 seconds but it is possible to change this to a value between 6 and 40 seconds. If a switch port doesn't receive BPDUs by the end of the max age limit, STP will re-converge by looking for an alternative path.

Portfast Technology

On Cisco switches, some ports connected to user nodes may not need to receive BPDUs and they need to transition to the forwarding state immediately. The portfast technology is a proprietary technology from Cisco that allows ports to immediately transition from blocking to forwarding state.

STP Convergence

To understand STP well, you must know the steps that a switch goes through after booting up until it reaches a full convergence. These steps include the following:

Step 1: Election of the root bridge.

Step 2: Election of root ports.

Step 3: Elect the designated and the non-designated ports.

The election of root bridge is done by sending BPDUs, and the switch that has the lowest BID will become the root bridge. The BID is made up of the MAC address of the device and the STP priority for that device.

Once the root bridge has been elected, the switches move into determining the root ports. These are the ports that mark the best paths to the root bridge. This depends on the bandwidth that is available on each link.

The designated ports are the non-root ports that switches can use to forward traffic to root bridge. Each link must have one designated port. All ports on a root bridge are designated ports. Once the ports have been elected, the STP will determine the links that are to be blocked.

The ports to be clocked are usually the ones that are not the root ports nor are they designated ports. These ports are marked as blocked and they will only be activated in case one of primary links fail.

Configuring STP

The default setting is that Cisco switches come with STP turned on. However, there are various other options for STP that we can configure.

As stated earlier, the Bit is made up of the MAC address and the priority of the switch. However, we cannot change the MAC address of a device, but the priority can be changed. However, this change is done per VLAN. There are two ways for doing this:

1. Using root primary and secondary
   We can use this for specification of the switch to be the root bridge and the one to be the secondary. The command should be run in global configuration mode. We use the following commands:
   spanning-tree vlan <VLAN_ID> root primary- for root bridge
   spanning-tree vlan <VLAN_ID> root secondary- for backup
2. Secondly, we can use the priority command. Spanning tree command is a BID with a value ranging between 0 and 61440. The priority is any number that lies in this range and in multiples of 4096. What does this mean? It means that a value such as 200 cannot be used as a priority.

The configuration of the command is also done per VLAN. Here is a command for that:

spanning-tree vlan <VLAN_ID> priority <0-61440 with increments of 4096>

By default, the spanning tree has a priority of 32778. Here is an example of the command:

spanning-tree vlan 1-255 priority 4096

You can run the command on the different switches you have on your LAN while changing the value of the priority.

Configuring the Portfast Technology

We can configure the portfast technology provided by Cisco on the access ports of our switches. You only need to run the following commands on the access ports of the switch:

interface <Interface-Name> <Interface-ID>

spanning-tree portfast

After executing the above command, the port will change its state from blocking to forwarding state and it will not send any BPDUs to these interfaces.

Verifying and Troubleshooting STP

You may be in need of verifying whether STP is working on the switches. Here are the commands that can be used for this purpose. Run the commands in the privileged EXEC mode:

show spanning-tree active - this command returns the active STP instances on your switch. Some parts of the output from this command include the STP type, the VLANs with STP, the roles and priority of ports and the bridge ID.

```
Switch#show spanning-tree active
VLAN0001
  Spanning tree enabled protocol ieee
  Root ID    Priority    32769
             Address     00D0.BC5A.9614
             This bridge is the root
             Hello Time  2 sec  Max Age 20 sec  Forward Delay 15 sec

  Bridge ID  Priority    32769  (priority 32768 sys-id-ext 1)
             Address     00D0.BC5A.9614
             Hello Time  2 sec  Max Age 20 sec  Forward Delay 15 sec
             Aging Time  20

Interface        Role Sts Cost      Prio.Nbr Type
---------------- ---- --- --------- --------
-------------------------------
Fa0/1            Desg FWD 19        128.1    P2p
Fa0/2            Desg FWD 19        128.2    P2p

Switch#
```

show spanning-tree summary - this command will give you all the details regarding what you need to know about STP so as to find the root bridge and the roles of other switches.

```
Switch#show spanning-tree summary
Switch is in pvst mode
Root bridge for: default
Extended system ID           is enabled
Portfast Default             is disabled
PortFast BPDU Guard Default  is disabled
Portfast BPDU Filter Default is disabled
Loopguard Default            is disabled
EtherChannel misconfig guard is disabled
UplinkFast                   is disabled
BackboneFast                 is disabled
Configured Pathcost method used is short

Name                 Blocking Listening Learning Forwarding STP Active
-------------------- -------- --------- -------- ---------- ----------
VLAN0001                    0         0        0          2          2

-------------------- -------- --------- -------- ---------- ----------
1 vlans                     0         0        0          2          2

Switch#
```

Other commands for STP verification and troubleshooting include the following:

- show spanning-tree detail
- show spanning-tree
- show spanning-tree vlan <VLAN-ID>
- show spanning-tree interface <Interface-ID>

Chapter 7

*I*nter-VLAN Routing

We previously stated that each VLAN runs on its own subnet, Switches are known to operate only at layer 2 of the OSI model, meaning that they don't observe logical addresses. This means that user nodes that are located on different nodes cannot communicate by default. To establish communication between such nodes, we need to implement inter-VLAN routing.

Inter-VLAN routing can be defined as a way of forwarding traffic from one VLAN to another VLAN by adding a router to the network. The purpose of VLANs is to segment a switch into various subnets. When a router is connected to the switch, we can configure it to exchange traffic between the various VLANs that are configured on the switch. The nodes on the VLANs will forward their traffic to the router which will in turn forward the traffic to the destination node regardless of the VLAN it is operating in.

We can implement inter-VLAN routing in two ways:

- Traditional inter-VLAN routing
- Router-on-a-stick

Traditional Inter-VLAN Routing

In this mechanism, a router is connected to a switch via multiple interfaces, one for every VLAN. The router interfaces are configured to be default gateways for the VLANs that are configured on the switch.

The ports connecting from the switch to the router are configured in the access mode in their respective LANs.

After a user node has sent a message to another node running on a different VLAN, the message will move from their node to the access port connecting to the router on their VLAN. Once the router has received the packet, it will examine the destination IP address of the packet then forward it to the correct network by use of the access port for destination VLAN.

The switch will be able to forward the frame to its destination since the router will have changed the VLAN information for the frame from the source VLAN to the destination VLAN.

When using the traditional inter-VLAN routing, the router is expected to have LAN interfaces that are as many as the number of VLANs that have been configured on the switch. This means that if 10 VLANs have been configured on the switch, the router should also have 10 interfaces.

We need to demonstrate how to configure the traditional inter-vlan routing on your network. Consider the topology given below:

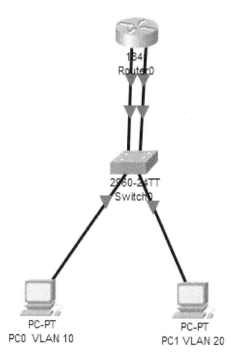

All VLANs are active and PCs have been assigned ports. Our configuration should be limited to the inter-VLAN configuration on the router and the switch ports that connect to the router *Router0*. Assign PC0 an IP address of 192.168.10.2 and a default gateway of 192.168.10.1. Assign PC1 an IP address of 192.168.20.3 and a default gateway of 192.168.20.1. Both should have a subnet mask of 255.255.255.0.

The fa0/0 interface on the router should belong to the VLAN. Assign it an IP address of 192.168.10.1 and a subnet mask of 255.255.255.0. The fa0/1 on the router should belong to VLAN 20, hence assign it an IP address of 192.168.20.1 and a subnet mask of 255.255.255.0.

First, we should configure the switch ports to access the right VLANs, the fa0/1 to access VLAN 10 and fa0/2 to access VLAN 20. We can accomplish this by running the following commands:

Switch>enable
Switch#config t
Enter configuration commands, one per line. End with CNTL/Z.
Switch(config)#int fa0/1
Switch(config-if)#switchport mode access
Switch(config-if)#switchport access vlan 10
Switch(config-if)#exit
Switch(config)#int fa0/2
Switch(config-if)#switchport mode access
Switch(config-if)#switchport access vlan 20
Switch(config-if)#exit
Switch(config)#

```
Switch>enable
Switch#config t
Enter configuration commands, one per line.  End with CNTL/Z.
Switch(config)#int fa0/1
Switch(config-if)#switchport mode access
Switch(config-if)#switchport access vlan 10
Switch(config-if)#exit
Switch(config)#int fa0/2
Switch(config-if)#switchport mode access
Switch(config-if)#switchport access vlan 20
Switch(config-if)#exit
Switch(config)#
```

My assumption is that you have already created the VLANs and assigned those names if possible. If you have not done so, just do it by running commands similar to the ones given below:

Switch(config-if)#vlan 10
Switch(config-vlan)#name FINANCE

Switch(config-vlan)#exit
Switch(config)#vlan 20
Switch(config-vlan)#name ICT
Switch(config-vlan)#exit
Switch(config)#exit

Once you have done the configuration, move to the privileged exec mode and save the changes by running this command:

copy running-config startup-config

```
Switch#copy running-config startup-config
Destination filename [startup-config]?
Building configuration...
[OK]
Switch#
```

We now need to configure the router with the default gateways that match those of the VLANs. The fa0/0 should have IP address 192.168.10.1/24 while fa0/1 interface should have IP address 192.168.20.1/24. This can be accomplished by running the following commands:

Router0(config)#int fa0/0
Router0(config-if)#ip address 192.168.10.1 255.255.255.0
Router0(config-if)#no shutdown
Router0(config-if)#
%LINK-5-CHANGED: Interface FastEthernet0/0, changed state to up
%LINEPROTO-5-UPDOWN: Line protocol on Interface FastEthernet0/0, changed state to up
Router0(config-if)#exit
Router0(config)#
Router0(config)#int fa0/1
Router0(config-if)#ip address 192.168.20.1 255.255.255.0
Router0(config-if)#no shutdown
Router0(config-if)#exit
Router0(config)#

```
Router0>enable
Password:
Password:
Router0#config t
Enter configuration commands, one per line.  End with CNTL/Z.
Router0(config)#int fa0/0
Router0(config-if)#ip address 192.168.10.1 255.255.255.0
Router0(config-if)#no shutdown

Router0(config-if)#
%LINK-5-CHANGED: Interface FastEthernet0/0, changed state to up

%LINEPROTO-5-UPDOWN: Line protocol on Interface FastEthernet0/0,
changed state to up

Router0(config-if)#exit
Router0(config)#
Router0(config)#int fa0/1
Router0(config-if)#ip address 192.168.20.1 255.255.255.0
Router0(config-if)#no shutdown
Router0(config-if)#exit
Router0(config)#|
```

You can then save the changes you have made on the switch. If you
ping the two PCs, they should be able to communicate with each
other even though they are on different VLANs.

Router-on-a-Stick

In this type of inter-VLAN routing mechanism, the router is
connected to the switch using one interface. The switchport that
connects to the router is configured as the *trunk link*. The router's
single interface connected to the switch is configured with multiple
IP addresses that corresponding to the VLANs created or configured
on the switch. The interface will accept traffic from all VLANs and
determine the correct destination of the traffic based on the source
and destination IP addresses of the packets.

The data is then forwarded to the switch with the right VLAN
information. This type of connection is demonstrated in the figure
given below:

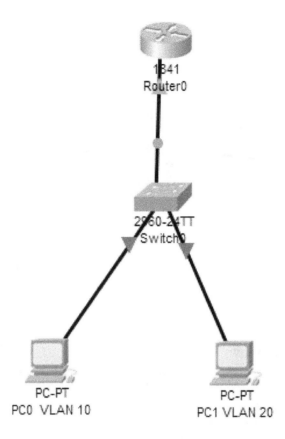

The interface that connects the router to the switch is the trunk link. The router will accept traffic that is tagged from VLANs on the switch via the trunk link. The physical interface on the router is then divided into smaller interfaces known as *sub interfaces*. Once the router has received the tagged traffic, it will forward the traffic out to the sub interface with the destination IP address.

Sub interfaces are not real interfaces but they rely on the LAN physical interfaces on a router for the purpose of forwarding data to the various VLANs. Every sub interface is configured using an IP address and assigned a VLAN depending on the design.

We now need to demonstrate how the configuration of inter-VLAN routing can be done using router-on-a-stick as opposed to using the traditional routing method. We have the following topology with more VLANs than the previous one:

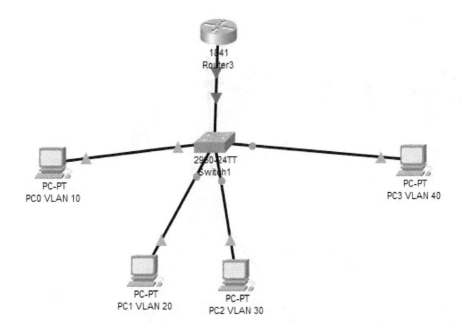

The topology shows four hosts located on 4 VLANs. The Native VLAN is the VLAN 99. The router is connected to fa0/1 interface of the switch, PC0 to fa0/2 interface of the switch, PC1 to fa0/3 interface of the switch, PC2 to fa0/4 interface of the switch while PC3 to the fa0/5 interface of the switch.

Assign the PCs the following IP addresses:

- PC0- 192.168.10.3
- PC1- 192.168.20.3
- PC2- 192.168.30.3
- PC4- 192.168.40.3

The PCs should also be assigned the following default gateways:

- PC0- 192.168.10.1
- PC1- 192.168.20.1
- PC2- 192.168.30.1
- PC4- 192.168.40.1

The subnet masks should all be set to 255.255.255.0.

Our job is to configure the router and the switch for inter-VLAN routing to ensure that devices from all VLANs can communicate with each other.

In the traditional inter-VLAN routing method, you realized that we assigned an IP address to the router interface that is connected to the switch. However, this is not done when using the router-on-a-stick method. We only have to implement the right configuration on the switchport fa0/1 which connects the switch to the router then configure the router correctly.

Step 1:

The first step is to define the port on witch1 that is connected to the router3 as *trunk link*. After that, traffic from all VLANs will be able to use that interface to reach the router. This can be done by running the following command:

Switch(config)#int fa0/1
Switch(config-if)#switchport mode trunk
Switch(config-if)#
Switch#

If you don't configure the above port as a trunk, you may encounter many errors.

Step 2:

We can do the configuration for inter-VLAN routing in this step on our router. As we had stated, when configuring router-on-a-stick, we rely on sub interfaces.
To create a sub interface, we use the interface_id.Sub interface_id command while in the global configuration mode. Note that there must be a dot (.) between the interface and the subinterface. The ID for the subinterface can be any logical number but it is recommended that it should describe the VLAN.

Note that the commands for creating the sub interfaces should be run on the router. Let us first create a subinterface for routing for VLAN 10, we run the command given below:

Router(config)#int fa 0/0.10

The above command will take us to subinterface configuration mode which is shown by the prompt shown below:

Router(config-subif)#

It is in this mode that we are able to link the VLAN ID to the interface and assign it an IP address and subnet mask.

Step 3:

We now need to link the above subinterface to the VLAN ID, which can be done by running the following command:

encapsulation dot1q <VLAN_ID>

The command will help us specify that the subinterface will be getting traffic from the specified VLAN. We can link VLAN 10 to this subinterface by running the command given below:

Router(config-subif)#encapsulation dot1q 10

Step 4:

We should now assign an IP address and a subnet mask to the subinterface and these will be used for the VLAN 10. For this, we will be suing the default gateways of the corresponding PCs as shown below:

Router(config-subif)#ip address 192.168.10.1 255.255.255.0

```
Router(config)#int fa 0/0.10
Router(config-subif)#encapsulation dot1q 10
Router(config-subif)#ip address 192.168.10.1 255.255.255.0
```

Step 5:

After assigning the sub interfaces to the respective VLANs, the LAN interfaces that they have been connected to should be activated by running the *no shutdown* command. This means that we run the following commands on the router:

Router(config)#int fa 0/0
Router(config-if)#no shutdown
Router(config-if)#
%LINK-5-CHANGED: Interface FastEthernet0/0, changed
state to up
%LINEPROTO-5-UPDOWN: Line protocol on Interface
FastEthernet0/0, changed state to up
%LINK-5-CHANGED: Interface FastEthernet0/0.10, changed
state to up
%LINEPROTO-5-UPDOWN: Line protocol on Interface
FastEthernet0/0.10, changed state to up
Router(config-if)#

The interface will be activated, allowing for the inter-VLAN routing
to take place.

We mentioned the native VLAN. What is it? This is the VLAN that
carries untagged traffic. To configure the subinterface for the native
VLAN, we run the following command on the router:

encapsulation dot1Q <Native_VLAN_ID> native

The use of the *native* keyword helps us mark the specified VLAN as
the native VLAN.

Note that we had already set the fa0/1 on the switch as the trunk link.
We had also configured the subinterface for VLAN 10. We now
need to configure the sub interfaces for the other VLANs. This can
be done by running the following commands:

Router>en
Router#config t
Enter configuration commands, one per line. End with CNTL/Z.
Router(config)#int fa 0/0.20
Router(config-subif)#
%LINK-5-CHANGED: Interface FastEthernet0/0.20, changed
state to up

%LINEPROTO-5-UPDOWN: Line protocol on Interface FastEthernet0/0.20, changed state to up
Router(config-subif)#encapsulation dot1Q 20
Router(config-subif)#ip address 192.168.20.3 255.255.255.0
Router(config-subif)#exit
Router(config)#int fa 0/0.30
Router(config-subif)#
%LINK-5-CHANGED: Interface FastEthernet0/0.30, changed state to up
%LINEPROTO-5-UPDOWN: Line protocol on Interface FastEthernet0/0.30, changed state to up
Router(config-subif)#encapsulation dot1Q 30
Router(config-subif)#ip address 192.168.30.3 255.255.255.0
Router(config-subif)#exit
Router(config)#int fa 0/0.40
Router(config-subif)#
%LINK-5-CHANGED: Interface FastEthernet0/0.40, changed state to up
%LINEPROTO-5-UPDOWN: Line protocol on Interface FastEthernet0/0.40, changed state to up
Router(config-subif)#encapsulation dot1Q 40
Router(config-subif)#ip address 192.168.40.3 255.255.255.0
Router(config-subif)#exit
Router(config)#int fa 0/0
Router(config-if)#no shutdown
Router(config-if)#exit
Router(config)#

```
Router>en
Router#config t
Enter configuration commands, one per line.  End with CNTL/Z.
Router(config)#int fa 0/0.20
Router(config-subif)#
%LINK-5-CHANGED: Interface FastEthernet0/0.20, changed state to up

%LINEPROTO-5-UPDOWN: Line protocol on Interface FastEthernet0/0.20, changed state to up

Router(config-subif)#encapsulation dot1Q 20|
Router(config-subif)#ip address 192.168.20.3 255.255.255.0
Router(config-subif)#exit
Router(config)#int fa 0/0.30
Router(config-subif)#
%LINK-5-CHANGED: Interface FastEthernet0/0.30, changed state to up

%LINEPROTO-5-UPDOWN: Line protocol on Interface FastEthernet0/0.30, changed state to up

Router(config-subif)#encapsulation dot1Q 30
Router(config-subif)#ip address 192.168.30.3 255.255.255.0
Router(config-subif)#exit
Router(config)#int fa 0/0.40
Router(config-subif)#
%LINK-5-CHANGED: Interface FastEthernet0/0.40, changed state to up

%LINEPROTO-5-UPDOWN: Line protocol on Interface FastEthernet0/0.40, changed state to up

Router(config-subif)#encapsulation dot1Q 40
Router(config-subif)#ip address 192.168.40.3 255.255.255.0
Router(config-subif)#exit
Router(config)#int fa 0/0
Router(config-if)#no shutdown
Router(config-if)#exit
Router(config)#
```

At this point, we should be able to communicate between the different VLANs configured on the switch. Run the *show ip route* command in the privileged exec mode of the switch and see whether the connection has been done:

```
Router>en
Router#show ip route
Codes: C - connected, S - static, I - IGRP, R - RIP, M - mobile, B - BGP
       D - EIGRP, EX - EIGRP external, O - OSPF, IA - OSPF inter area
       N1 - OSPF NSSA external type 1, N2 - OSPF NSSA external type 2
       E1 - OSPF external type 1, E2 - OSPF external type 2, E - EGP
       i - IS-IS, L1 - IS-IS level-1, L2 - IS-IS level-2, ia - IS-IS inter area
       * - candidate default, U - per-user static route, o - ODR
       P - periodic downloaded static route

Gateway of last resort is not set

C    192.168.10.0/24 is directly connected, FastEthernet0/0.10
C    192.168.20.0/24 is directly connected, FastEthernet0/0.20
C    192.168.30.0/24 is directly connected, FastEthernet0/0.30
C    192.168.40.0/24 is directly connected, FastEthernet0/0.40

Router#
```

You can issue the ping command between the various VLANs on the different VLANs and they should be able to communicate.

Chapter 8

OSPF

OSPF stands for *Open Shortest Path First*. It is a classless Link State routing protocol that uses areas to scale better.

OSPF falls under the category of link-state routing protocols. These types of protocols work by calculating the cost along the path from the source network to destination network using the SPF (Shortest Path First) algorithm.

OSPF Packets

OSPF supports 5 different types of packets including the following:

1. Hello- this forms the first packet sent by routers that have been configured with the OSPF algorithm. This is done using the multicast IP address that is reserved for OSPF, which is normally 224.0.0.5. The hello packets helps the routers discover their neighbors and establish relationships.
   In point to point and multicast networks, hello packets are
   For NBMA networks, this is done after 30 seconds.
   The hello packets serve the following three tasks in OSPF algorithm:
   • Discovering and establishing neighbor adjacencies.
   • Advertising the OSPF parameters that are needed to form neighbor relationships.
   • Election of DR (Designated Router) and BDR (Backup Designated Router) in the multi-access networks.
2. DBD (Database Description) - this is a packet with a list of routes that have been learnt by a router in a particular routing domain. Once a router has received this packet, it has to check the list against its link-state database for the purpose of discovering any missing routes.
3. Link State Request (LSR) - when a router that it has missing routes from the information contained in the DBD packet that it has received, it has to send this packet to the router that has informed it of the missing routes requesting it to provide information regarding the missing routes.

4. LSU (Link State Update) - this is a packet send by a router that has the information about the missing routes. It has more details regarding a certain route, such as next-hop information and the cost of reaching a particular route that was requested via LSR.
5. LSAck (Link State Acknowledgement)- this packet is sent for confirming that the router has received an LSU.

Dijkstra's algorithm, metric and administrative distance

As we stated earlier, OSPF relies on the SPF algorithm. The OSPF link state database of the router has information known as MAP which is used for calculation of the best path leading to a remote network. However, the OSPF algorithm doesn't keep the backup paths to routes. However, when a route leading to a network goes down, the SPF algorithm is executed again to determine the alternate or backup path to the route.

OSPF has an administrative distance of 110. This explains why it is preferred compared to other routing protocols like RIP, but it is not much as trusted as EIGRP, static routes and the directly connected routes.

Cost is the metric used in OSPF. This refers to the bandwidth on every link or the cost that has been configured by the administrator *via ip ospf cost* command.

Configuring OSPF

To enable the OSPF protocol on your router, you must enter the global configuration mode of the router and run the following command:

router ospf <process-ID>

The process-ID is a logically significant number whose value ranges between 1 and 65535. The number is locally significant meaning that it will only identify the OSPF process that is running on the router. In our demonstration, we will be using one process-ID to maintain consistency. Suppose we have the topology shown below:

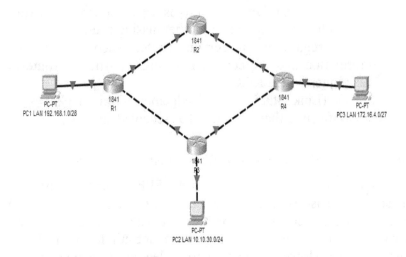

PC1 LAN 192.168.1.0/28

PC3 LAN 172.16.4.0/27

PC2 LAN 10.10.30.0/24

There are four routers in the network, that is, R1 to R4. Three LAN segments have been connected to the routers R1, R3 and R4. To enable OSPF on the routers, we should run the following command in the global configuration mode of the routers:

router ospf <process-ID>

The process-ID should be a logically significant number with the value ranging between 1 and 655365. By logically significant we mean that the number will only identify the OSPF process that is running on the router. In this case, we need to use the value 10 as the process-ID on all routers. Run the following command on the router R1:

Router(config)#router ospf 10
Router(config-router)#

After running the above command, we are taken to the OSPF configuration mode as shown above. It is in this mode that we are able to configure the OSPF options that we need. In OSPF, we use the *network* command for the purpose of advertising routes. The command takes the syntax given below:

router(config-router)#network <network-address> <wildcard-mask> area <area-ID>

OSPF relies on areas, and all routers in one area share a map. In our case, we need to deal only with the backbone area named *area 0*, meaning that all our switches will be in this area. As a network grows in size, multiple-areas should be introduced so as to reduce the map size.

Wildcard Mask

This is simply the inverse of a subnet mask. To calculate it, first write down the subnet mask of broadcast address which is normally 255.255.255.255. This is simply the broadcast address for the zero networks. Next, write down the subnet mask of the network or IP address in question. You can then get the difference between the two by subtracting the values of network's subnet mask from the 255.255.255.255 subnet mask.

During the determination of the network to advertise by the router, values of "0" are ignored while values that are above that are ignored. Suppose we need to advertise a network of 192.168.1.0/27. Only routes that match the first three octets will be advertised by the router but the values in the fourth octet will be ignored.

Only the directly connected networks that we need to use OSPF are advertised. If we need to advertise the network 192.168.1.0/28 in OSPF, we can run the following command on the router R1:

Router(config-router)#network 192.168.1.0 0.0.0.15 area 0

```
Router(config)#router ospf 10
Router(config-router)#network 192.168.1.0 0.0.0.15 area 0
```

This means that in the topology, we should advertise all directly connected networks on each router. In router one for example, we should advertise three networks. These include:

- The network where PC1 is located. We have advertised this in the above command.
- The network in the link connecting routers R1 to R2.
- The network in the link connecting routers R1 to R3.

This means that on the router R1, we should run the following commands:

Router(config)#router ospf 10
Router(config-router)#network 192.168.10.0.0.0.15 area 0
Router(config-router)#network 192.168.12.0.0.0.3 area 0
Router(config-router)#network 192.168.13.4.0.0.3 area 0
Router(config-router)#

The same should also be done on the other routers so that they may advertise the networks that are connected to them. Note that before running the commands, you must calculate the wildcards first. To configure the router ID, the command should be executed in router configuration mode. To set this to 1.1.1.1 for the router R1, we only run the following command:

Router(config)#router ospf 10
Router(config-router)#router-id 1.1.1.1

```
Router#config t
Enter configuration commands, one per line.  End with CNTL/Z.
Router(config)#router ospf 10
Router(config-router)#router-id 1.1.1.1
Router(config-router)#
```

Make sure that you do the same for other routers while assigning them unique IDs.

Loopback Interfaces

This is simply a virtual interface, meaning that it only exists on the router and it is not connected to other physical devices. It gets to UP immediately it is configured. It is configured via this command:

interface <loopback> <Loopback_interface_number>

After running the command, you will be taken to interface configuration in which you will be able to configure the interface options like IP address. The following shows how to configure some loopback interface on the router R1 and assign it an IP address:

Router(config)#interface loopback 0

Router(config-if)#ip address 172.16.1.1 255.255.255.0

To see the OSPF details and troubleshoot issues with the OSPF, run the following command:

Router#show ip ospf neighbor

Conclusion

This marks the end of this guide. You are now equipped with all the skills that are necessary for you to pass the exam. There are various types of networks which are determined by the amount of area that they cover. Networking standards are essential in networking. Network standards help ensure that network hardware and software work together. Without such standards, it would be difficult to develop a network for sharing information. These standards are usually developed by both governments and industry organizations.

Network cables provide a medium for transmission of data from one network device to another. There are various types of network cabling that can choose for your network. This will be determined by a number of factors including the nature of the environment and the amount of money you are ready and willing to spend in network cabling.

IP addresses help us to identify network devices uniquely. There are two types of IP addresses, IPV4 and IPV6. IPV4 addresses are common and they have been in use for a long period of time. IPV6 addresses were developed to help cater for the increasing demand for IP addresses as the internet grows in size every day.

The hierarchical network design is recommended by CISCO as it provides an easier way of defining the roles of various nodes in the network. With VLANS, a single switch can be divided into a number of subnets. Computers in various departments can be configured to run in different subnets. Communication between VLANs is possible. This can be achieved through inter-VLAN routing whereby a router is added to the switch to manage traffic coming from different VLANs.